A Note to Parents

DK READERS is a compelling program for beginning readers, designed in conjunction with leading literacy experts, including Dr. Linda Gambrell, Professor of Education at Clemson University. Dr. Gambrell has served as President of the National Reading Conference and the College Reading Association, and has recently been elected to serve as President of the International Reading Association.

Beautiful illustrations and superb full-color photographs combine with engaging, easy-to-read stories and informational texts to offer a fresh approach to each subject in the series. Each DK READER is guaranteed to capture a child's interest while developing his or her reading skills, general knowledge, and love of reading.

The five levels of DK READERS are aimed at different reading abilities, enabling you to choose the books that are exactly right for your child:

Pre-level 1: Learning to read
Level 1: Beginning to read
Level 2: Beginning to read alone
Level 3: Reading alone
Level 4: Proficient readers

The "normal" age at which a child begins to read can be anywhere from three to eight years old. Adult participation through the lower levels is very helpful for providing encouragement, discussing storylines, and sounding out unfamiliar words.

No matter which level you select, you can be sure that you are helping your child learn to read, then read to learn!

LONDON, NEW YORK,
MELBOURNE, MUNICH, and DELHI

For DK/BradyGames
Publisher David Waybright
Editor-in-Chief H. Leigh Davis
Licensing Director Mike Degler
International Translations
Brian Saliba
Title Manager Tim Fitzpatrick

For DK Publishing
Publishing Director Beth Sutinis
Licensing Editor Nancy Ellwood

Reading Consultant
Linda B. Gambrell, Ph.D.

Produced by
Shoreline Publishing Group LLC
President James Buckley Jr.
Designer Tom Carling, carlingdesign.com

DK/BradyGAMES
800 East 96th St., 3rd floor
Indianapolis, IN 46240

09 10 11 10 9 8 7 6 5 4 3 2

A catalog record for this book is available from the Library of Congress.

ISBN: 978-0-7566-4432-1 (Paperback)
ISBN: 978-0-7566-4479-6(Hardback)

Printed and bound by Lake Book

Discover more at
www.dk.com

DK READERS

BEGINNING TO READ ALONE
2

Meet Ash

Written by Michael Teitelbaum

DK
DK Publishing

Ash Ketchum is a 10-year-old boy from Pallet Town. And, just like you, he loves Pokémon. Ash wants to become the world's greatest Pokémon Trainer.

He knows the journey he must take will be a long one. He will have to catch Pokémon. Then he will have to train them. It will take time and a lot of effort. But Ash is willing to put in the hard work it takes.

Along the way, he will meet many amazing people. It will be a really big adventure!

Ash Ketchum and Pikachu

Ash begins his journey at the lab of Professor Oak. Pokémon Trainers who are from Pallet Town start there.

Professor Oak gives new Trainers their first Pokémon. He usually gives them a Bulbasaur, a Charmander, a Squirtle, or a Pikachu. He explains that Trainers must care for their

Professor Oak

Pokémon. Each Pokémon is different. Some are big. Some are small. Each one has its own skills. Each one likes to live in a different sort of place. It will be important for Ash to be friends with his Pokémon.

But which Pokémon will Ash choose to begin his journey?

Professor Oak's lab

Ash meets Pikachu

The big day finally comes. Ash will meet Professor Oak. He will get his first Pokémon.

But Ash doesn't get there in time. He sleeps too late!

When Ash finally gets to Professor Oak's lab, only Pikachu is left. So Ash chooses Pikachu, a small, yellow Electric-type Pokémon.

Pikachu can be shy and sometimes stubborn. Pikachu can be hard to train. But Ash saves Pikachu when Pikachu is in danger. Ash proves that he cares. A great friendship begins!

Ash starts his Pokémon journey. He leaves Pallet Town with Pikachu by his side. He is also traveling with his friend Misty. Now Ash has to catch his first Pokémon out in the wild. What will he catch first?

Ash spots a Caterpie. Here's his big chance. He makes his move. Ash catches the Caterpie. He is very proud. He has captured his first wild Pokémon.

Team Rocket

On Ash's journey, he will meet
some people who want to take his
Pokémon. Team Rocket tries to steal
Pikachu! But Ash's Caterpie saves
the day for its new Pokémon Trainer.
It uses its String Shot to stop Team
Rocket.

Brock, Ash, Misty,
Pikachu, Onix,
and Togepi

Ash visits cities on his journey. Every
major city has a Pokémon gym.
Each gym has a Gym Leader. The
Gym Leader is an expert Pokémon
Trainer. If you and your Pokémon

defeat a Gym Leader, you earn a special badge.

Ash goes to the Pewter City Gym. There he battles the Gym Leader, Brock. Brock's Pokémon are Geodude and Onix. Ash defeats Brock to earn the Boulder Badge. Ash and Brock also become friends. Ash is on his way now. And he has made a new friend, too!

Pokémon Badges

Pokémon Trainers try to defeat gym leaders in battle. If they do, they earn a badge from that leader's gym. Trainers try to earn badges from each gym in a league. If they do, they get to compete in that league's tournament. *Knuckle Badge*

Gary Oak is Professor Oak's grandson. He grew up next door to Ash back in Pallet Town.

Gary is a Pokémon Trainer, too. But all Gary cares about is how many Pokémon he catches.

Ash thought it was important to catch more Pokémon than Gary. Then Ash learned that caring for your Pokémon is more important than how many Pokémon you have. He also found out that a Trainer teaches his Pokémon and also learns from them.

Squirtle, Gary's first Pokémon

Zubat

Ash has made some good friends during his Pokémon journey. Ash's friend Brock is an older and more experienced Pokémon Trainer. Brock is the Pewter City Gym Leader. His favorite Pokémon are Rock-type Pokémon, like Onix and Geodude.

Misty is one of Ash's best friends. She is a super Pokémon Trainer. Misty is also the Gym Leader of the Cerulean City Gym. Misty loves training Water-type Pokémon. Her favorites are Staryu, Starmie, and Goldeen.

Misty loves Water-type Pokémon.

Ash travels to many regions on his Pokémon journey. When he was in the Sinnoh region, he met Dawn. They became friends. Dawn got her Pokémon from Professor Rowan. Her first Pokémon was a Piplup.

Ash also became friends with May. May wants

May and Torchic

Regions of the Pokémon World

The Pokémon world is divided into many regions. Ash is from the Kanto region. Dawn is from the Sinnoh region. Other regions include Johto, Hoenn, and the Orange Islands. Each region is different. Each one has its own Pokémon and Pokémon contests—and new adventures await in all of them!

to compete in Pokémon contests and win ribbons. May loves cute Pokémon, like Torchic, Wurmple, and Eevee.

Cissy's gym in the Orange Islands

Ash travels in the Orange Islands. The Orange Islands have their own Pokémon League with their own rules. They have their own Pokémon gyms and Pokémon Centers.

The Orange Islands include Valencia Island, Tangelo Island,

Murcott Island, and Mikan Island. In the Orange Islands, Ash learns that friendship, trust, loyalty, and teamwork are the most important parts of being a Pokémon Trainer.

Ash also competes in the Orange Island gyms.

Luana is an Orange Island Gym Leader.

Danny is an Orange Island Gym Leader.

There are four Orange Island gyms. The four Gym Leaders are known as the Orange Crew.

If a Pokémon Trainer can defeat all four Gym Leaders, he or she wins the Orange Trophy. These Gym Leaders are all great Trainers.

In the Mikan Island Gym, Ash battles Cissy for the Coral-Eye Badge. In the Navel Island Gym, Ash battles Danny for the Sea Ruby Badge. In the Trovita Island Gym, Ash battles Rudy for the Spikeshell Badge. In the Kumquat Island Gym, Ash battles Luana for the Jade Star Badge.

Ash won these Orange Island badges.

Dawn and her Pokémon

When Ash travels in the Sinnoh region, he meets a new friend named Dawn. They start in Twinleaf Town.

Twinleaf Town is where Dawn grew up. Their next stop is Jubilife City. It is the biggest city in the Sinnoh region. It has a Poké Mart. Jubilife City also holds a Pokémon contest for Trainers.

In Floaroma Town, Ash cheers as Dawn wins her first ribbon. Oreburgh City has a Pokémon gym. If you can beat Roark, the Oreburgh City Gym Leader, you'll earn a Coal Badge.

Cranidos, one of Roark's Rock-type Pokémon

Ash is learning a lot on his Pokémon journey. He learns that he must always use his Pokémon's own abilities. He must never push his Pokémon too hard.

As Trainers compete side by side with their Pokémon, their friendship grows. And they learn more about each other. Ash also learns that a Pokémon Trainer is only as good as

Pokémon Evolution
Pokémon can "evolve." This means they grow and change into a new form. An evolved Pokémon can have new and stronger powers.

his or her Pokémon. Trainers must
listen to their Pokémon. They must
feel what is in their hearts.

Of course, everyone knows about Ash's Pikachu. Pikachu is one of the most famous Pokémon. But Ash has other Pokémon too.

Bulbasaur

Bulbasaur is a Grass-type Pokémon. It has a seed on its back. It uses the seed for food. Bulbasaur evolves into Ivysaur and Venusaur.

Squirtle is a Water-type Pokémon. It hides in its shell. Then it attacks by squirting water. Squirtle evolves into Wartortle and then into Blastoise.

Buizel is a Water-type
Pokémon. It is a great
swimmer.
Buizel can float
on the water. Buizel
evolves into Floatzel.

Buizel

Gligar is a Ground-and-Flying-type
Pokémon. It has wings so it can
fly. It sails along, riding the wind.
Gligar's sharp
claws make
it dangerous
during a battle.
Gligar evolves
into Gliscor.

Gligar

Ash is always looking for more Pokémon. He works hard to become the best Pokémon Trainer he can be. He knows that a Trainer and his or her Pokémon must work together. They must learn from each other. Pokémon have strong wills, just like people. Trainers must learn to respect their Pokémon's will.

And so Ash's Pokémon journey continues.

Who knows? One day he may reach his goal—to be the world's greatest Pokémon Trainer!

More of Ash's Pokémon

Ash Ketchum has had a long, fun journey. He has met many awesome Pokémon Trainers. He has also caught dozens of Pokémon! He spends the most time with Pikachu, of course. Many other Pokémon work with him often. Here are a few more Pokémon that travel with Ash.

Charizard

Cyndaquil

Corphish

Torkoal